A New True Book

BUTTERFLIES AND MOTHS

By James P. Rowan

This "true book" was prepared
under the direction of
Illa Podendorf,
formerly with the Laboratory School,
University of Chicago

 CHILDRENS PRESS, CHICAGO

D1122855

Comma butterfly

Dedicated to Jan

PHOTO CREDITS

Lynn Stone—2, 7 (right), 13 (right), 15 (left), 16 (right), 17 (2 photos), 20, 39, 40 (bottom right), 43 (top and bottom right), 44 (top)

Kjell B. Sandved—Cover, 9 (3 photos), 10 (3 photos, top left, right, and middle left), 15 (right), 21, 27

Jim Rowan—6 (left), 10, (2 photos middle & bottom right), 13 (left), 16 (left), 19, 24 (2 photos), 25, 28, 29, 31, 37 (2 photos), 38 (2 photos), 40 (top and bottom left)

Jerry Hennen—23, 32, 34, 36, 43 (bottom left), 44 (2 photos bottom), 45

Charles M. Hogue, Ph.D—4

USDA: United States Department of Agriculture—6 (right)

COVER—Papilio butterfly, Brazil

Library of Congress Cataloging in Publication Data

Rowan, James P.
   Butterflies and moths.

   (A New true book)
   Includes index.
   Summary: Discusses the characteristics and natural history of the scaly-winged insects of the order Lepidoptera.
   1. Butterflies—Juvenile literature. 2. Moths—Juvenile literature. [1. Butterflies. 2. Moths]
I. Title.
QL544.2.R68 1983   595.78   83-7216
ISBN 0-516-01692-X   AACR2

TABLE OF CONTENTS

Butterflies, Moths, and Other
   Insects... 5

Life Cycles... 12

Warning Colors and
   Look-alikes... 18

Looking Like Something Else... 25

Other Kinds of Protection... 29

Migration and Hibernation... 33

Studying Butterflies
   and Moths... 37

Words You Should Know... 46

Index... 47

Green fruit beetle

BUTTERFLIES, MOTHS, AND OTHER INSECTS

There are almost a million different kinds of insects in the world. Scientists divide all insects into groups called orders. There are about thirty-five different orders of insects.

Each order is made up of insects that are alike. For example, all beetles are in one order.

Young grasshopper

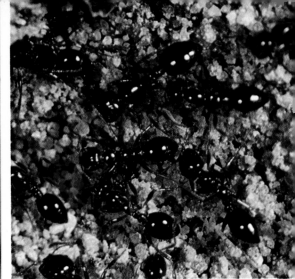
Carpentar ants

Grasshoppers, katydids,
and crickets are alike and
are in one order. Bees,
wasps, and ants are in one
order, and so are all flies.

Butterflies and moths
have their own order, too.
It is called the order
Lepidoptera.

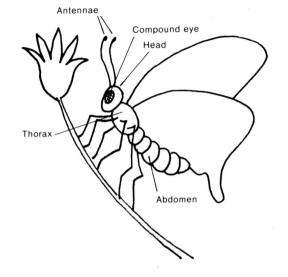

Antennae
Compound eye
Head
Thorax
Abdomen

Gulf fritillary. This kind
of butterfly is usually
orange with black spots
on the upper side of both
wings and silver spotted
on the underside
of the hind wing.

Butterflies and moths,
like all other insects, have
three parts to their
bodies—the head, the
thorax, and the abdomen.
They also have six legs
and two antennae.

7

Butterflies and moths are different from other insects in one way. They have large wings covered with thousands of tiny scales. The name *Lepidoptera* means scaly-wing in Greek.

Scales give color to the wings of butterflies and moths. They are very loosely attached to the wings. If the wings are

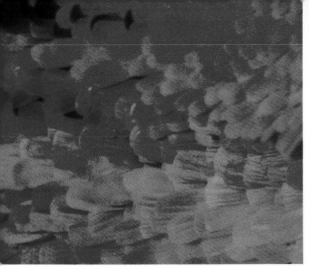

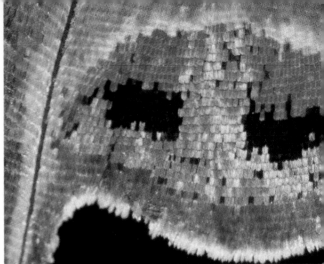

Close-ups of the wings of butterflies (top right and bottom) and a moth (top left).

touched, the scales come off. If all of the scales were removed, the wings would be perfectly clear.

9

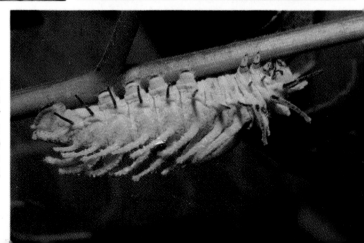

Top right: Nymphalida
Vanessa io from France
Top left: Moth from Ecuador
Middle right: Stenoma moth
Middle left: Morpho
butterfly from Peru
Right: Atlas Moth larva

Butterflies and moths are found all over the world. They live in forests, deserts, prairies, jungles, and even in the Arctic.

They come in all different sizes. Some can be very small, like the clothes moth. It is only about one quarter of an inch long. Some can be very big. The atlas moth of Asia has a wingspread of ten inches. It is one of the largest insects in the world.

LIFE CYCLES

All insects begin life as eggs. When some insects hatch from eggs, they look like tiny adults. As they grow, the young continue to look like adults. Eventually, many grow wings and fly. The grasshopper has a life cycle like this. A young insect with this kind of life cycle is called a nymph. Butterflies and moths,

Above: Cecropia caterpillar
Left: Linden looper larva

however, have a different kind of life cycle. When the egg of a butterfly or moth hatches, the young looks very different from the adult. It looks like a very small worm with short legs. It is called a caterpillar or larva.

The larva does nothing but eat. It grows bigger and bigger until it is full size. Then it enters a third stage called the pupa.

Sometimes a caterpillar spins a silk covering around itself for protection during the pupa stage. This covering is called a cocoon. Many kinds of moth caterpillars spin cocoons. The silkworm moth from Asia makes a cocoon so strong that people have been using it to make silk cloth for hundred of years.

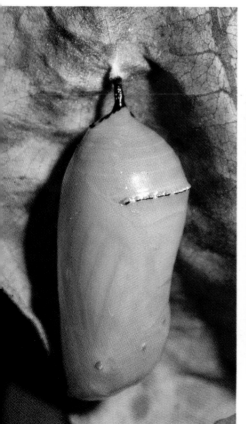

Below: Giant Silkworm moth from New Guinea
Left: Monarch chrysalis or pupa.Usually butterfly pupae hang upside down without external covering.

When a caterpillar is in the pupa stage, a great change takes place. The wormlike caterpillar turns into an adult butterfly or moth with four large wings and six long legs. Even the mouthparts are different. The caterpillar had

Right: Caterpillar of cecropia moth eating a leaf.
Below: Polyphemus moth larva

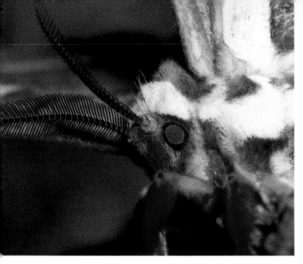

Above: Cecropia moth depositing eggs
Left: Close-up of the head of cecropia moth

strong jaws for chewing leaves. But the adult has mouthparts that coil up under its head like a spring. It can extend these mouthparts into flowers to sip up the nectar.

After mating the female butterfly or moth will lay eggs and start a new life cycle.

WARNING COLORS AND LOOK-ALIKES

Some butterflies and moths do not taste good to birds and other insect-eating animals. Sometimes these bad-tasting insects are brightly colored as a warning not to eat them.

One of these is the monarch butterfly. It is bright orange with black stripes and white spots. If a bird were to eat a

Monarch butterfly

monarch butterfly, it would
find out how badly it tasted.
The next time that bird
saw a monarch, it probably
would not eat it. It would
recognize the bright color
pattern and remember how
badly the last one tasted.

19

Viceroy butterfly

There is a butterfly called the viceroy butterfly that looks very much like the monarch. This butterfly tastes good to birds. But because it looks so much like the monarch, birds will not eat it. When one kind of animal looks like another kind, it is called mimicry.

Some butterflies and moths look like other kinds of insects altogether. The bumblebee sphinx moth looks like a large bumblebee as it flies around flowers. This protects it from being eaten by birds, who are afraid of being stung.

Sphinx moth from Venezuela

Some butterflies and moths even look like larger animals. The owl butterfly from South America has a very large spot on the underside of each hind wing. When it rests on a branch, it sits upside down and spreads its wings. To an insect-eating bird or lizard, it looks just like the two large, staring eyes of an owl. In the United States, the polyphemus moth has a similar pattern

Polyphemus moth

of eye spots on its hind wings.

The caterpillars of some butterflies and moths look like other animals, too. The tiger swallowtail caterpillar has two large spots on its back that look like eyes. If it is disturbed, it arches its

Tiger swallowtail

Black swallowtail larva

back to give the appearance
of a snake. To complete
this act, it sticks out from
its head a pair of bright
red horns that look like a
snake's tongue. And if all
this doesn't frighten an
enemy, the horns give off a
very bad odor to discourage
anything from eating it.

Geometrid moth blends into the background.

LOOKING LIKE SOMETHING ELSE

Some butterflies and moths are colored to look like the place they live so that they cannot be seen by their enemies.

Underwing moths look like the bark of the trees

that they rest on. These moths have brightly marked hind wings with red and black bands. They are easily seen when flying. When the moths rest on a tree trunk, the bright colors are hidden by the front wings, which look like the tree's bark.

There are some butterflies that look like dead leaves. The dead leaf butterfly from Asia has bright blue color on the

Can you find the moth resting on a dead leaf in Brazil?

top side of its wings. It, too, is easily seen when flying. But when it lands on a branch, it hides the bright color. It then shows only the back side of its wings, which are the color and shape of a dead leaf. In North America angle-wing butterflies also look like dead leaves when resting.

The caterpillars of geometrid moths look like branches with buds on them.

When an animal is colored to look like its background, it is camouflaged.

Geometrid
moth larva

Eastern
tent
caterpillars

OTHER KINDS
OF PROTECTION

Webworms and tent
caterpillars live together in
large groups. Together they
spin coverings of silk
around branches in a tree.
This is called a tent. During
the day these caterpillars

stay inside this tent for protection from their enemies. At night when it is safer, they leave the tent to feed on the leaves of the tree. As these caterpillars grow, they make the tent larger and larger. Sometimes the tent will be three or four feet across.

Some caterpillars are covered with long hairs or spines that make them

Woolly bear caterpillar

look bad to eat. The woolly
bear caterpillar has
thousands of long hairs
that cover its body from
end to end. A bird might
have a hard time eating a
caterpillar like this, so it is
usually left alone.

Saddle back caterpillar looks dangerous.

The tomato worm, the caterpillar of a large moth, has a large spine on its tail end. It looks dangerous but is in fact completely harmless. It sometimes fools birds. They may avoid the tomato worm because it looks so dangerous.

MIGRATION AND HIBERNATION

Once a caterpillar becomes an adult butterfly or moth, it is at the end of its life cycle. Most adults live for only several weeks. A few adults, however, can live for more than a year.

Some butterflies fly south for the winter as birds do. Monarch butterflies gather in huge flocks in the early autumn and fly to southern

Monarch
butterflies
migrate

California or Mexico before winter comes. This is called a migration.

Some long-lived adults stay north during the winter. They have to find a place for protection against the cold. There they go into a deep, sleeplike state called hibernation.

The mourning cloak butterfly may hibernate in a hollow log. When the temperature rises in the spring, the mourning cloak will warm up and fly once again. Sometimes it is warm enough in late February or early March so that this butterfly can be seen flying when snow is still on the ground.

Other kinds of butterflies and moths hibernate in caves or even in people's houses and garages.

Moth hibernating in cave

Left: Art Maraldi, an entomologist (a person who studies insects), works on his collection.
Right: Close-up of a moth on a spreading board.

STUDYING BUTTERFLIES AND MOTHS

Some people collect butterflies and moths. Sometimes they will trade them with collectors from other parts of the world.

Butterflies displayed in a case

Display case holding butterflies

You can see butterflies and moths from other countries in museums. Some large museums have many thousands of butterflies and moths in their collections.

Butterflies and moths can be collected in many different places. In the

White peacock

Black swallowtail (above), sulphur butterfly (bottom left),
and Painted lady (bottom right)

summer, they can be found in fields and prairies where there are flowers. In forests, some moths will be found resting on the trunks of trees. You must look for them carefully because many are colored like the bark of the trees. At night, a great variety of moths will be found flying around lights.

Another way to study butterflies and moths is to collect the caterpillars and raise them to be adults. They can be kept in large jars or wire cages. It is important to feed the caterpillars the same kind of leaves that they are found on. Most caterpillars eat only a single kind of plant and will starve if given a different kind.

Queen butterfly

Black witch moth (left) and
a Monarch caterpillar eating
milkweed leaf (below)

Zebra butterfly

Imperial moth (below left)
and Harris checkerspot
butterfly (right)

Red admiral
butterfly

Eventually, a caterpillar will turn into a pupa and then into an adult. If the adult is not going to be kept for a collection, it should be set free.

Butterflies and moths are beautiful creatures. Studying them can be interesting and educational. It is a hobby that fascinates people all over the world.

WORDS YOU SHOULD KNOW

abdomen(AB • duh • men) — the back end of an insect's body

antenna(an • TEN • ah) — one of a pair of long, thin feelers on an insect's head

camouflage(KAM • ah • flaje) — to hide with colors and patterns that look like the surroundings

coil(KOYL) — to wind around

hibernate(HI • ber • nait) — to spend the winter asleep in a protected place

larva(LAR • vah) — an insect that was hatched from an egg

migrate(MY • grate) — to move regularly to a different place at a certain time of year

mimicry(MIM • ik • kree) — to look like another animal; a copy

nectar(NEK • ter) — a sweet liquid found in many flowers

nymph(NIMF) — a young insect that has not yet developed into an adult

pupa(PYOO • pa) — the third stage in an insect's life in which it rests while it changes from a larva into an adult

spine(SPYNE) — a part of a plant or animal that sticks out with a sharp point

thorax(THOR • ax) — the middle part of an insect's body

transform(TRANSS • form) — to change

INDEX

abdomen, 7
angle-wing butterflies, 27-28
antennae, 7
ants, 6
Arctic, 11
Asia, 11, 15, 26
atlas moths, 11
bark, moths that resemble, 25, 26, 41
bee, 6, 21
beetles, 5
birds, 18-22, 31, 32
body parts, 7
bumblebees, 21
bumblebee sphinx moths, 21,
California, 34
camouflaged animals, 28
caterpillars, 13, 14, 16, 23, 28, 29-32, 33, 42, 45
clothes moths, 11
cocoons, 14, 15
collecting butterflies and moths, 37-45
colors, warning, 18-20

crickets, 6
dead leaf butterflies, 26
eggs, 12, 13, 17
flies, 6
geometrid moths, 28
grasshoppers, 6, 12
hairs, 30, 31
head, 7
hibernation, 34-36
insect orders, 5, 6
katydids, 6
larva, 13, 14
leaves, butterflies that resemble, 26-28
legs, 7, 16
Lepidoptera, 6, 8
life cycles, 12, 17, 33,
life spans, 33
lizards, 22
look-alikes, 21-24
Mexico, 34
migration, 33, 34
mimicry, 20
monarch butterflies, 18-20, 33

moth caterpillars, 14
mourning cloak butterflies, 35
mouthparts, 16, 17
museums, 39
North America, 27
nymphs, 12
order of butterflies and moths, 6
orders of insects, 5, 6
owl butterflies, 22
owls, 22
polyphemus moths, 22
pupa stage, 14, 16, 45
scales on wings, 8, 9
silkworm moths, 14-15
South America, 22

spines, 30, 32
studying butterflies and moths,
   37-45
tent caterpillars, 29
tents (spun protection), 29, 30
thorax, 7
tiger swallowtail butterflies, 23
tomato worms, 32
underwing moths, 25
United States, 22
viceroy butterflies, 20
wasps, 6
webworms, 29
wings, 8, 9, 12, 16, 22, 23, 26, 27
woolly bear caterpillars, 31

About the Author

James P. Rowan majored in zoology and geology at Northeastern Illinois University. He is currently a keeper in the reptile house at Lincoln Park Zoo in Chicago, Illinois. A professional photographer, Jim and his wife Jan have traveled around the world photographing animals, insects, and nature. He has more than forty thousand images on file and is adding hundreds of new subjects to his collection each year. His photographs have been published in a number of encyclopedias, textbooks, and magazines.